Cooking with Papi
Everyday Strategies for Raising Great Kids

By
Gary Surdam

> **Dedication:**
> *I dedicate this book to my wife, Millie, for her constant support and believing in my dreams.*
>
> *My children, Raquel, Joseph, James and Rianna for the inspiration behind this book
> and the hours of love we share in the kitchen.*

Special Thanks to:

Kenny Liang for the Chinese Translation

James Surdam for Cover Design

Cooking with Papi

Table of Contents

- Introduction

- Communication
    The recipe for connecting with your child

- Cooking with Raquel and Rianna

    Green Chili and Pork
    Refried Beans
    Spanish Rice
    Tortilla Treats

- Planning and Decision Making
    Make list, buy ingredients, reap rewards

- Cooking with James

    Wonton Chicken Salad
    Chicken Avocado Egg Rolls
    Wonton Treats

- Boundaries and Discipline
    Without rules, there is baking chaos

- Cooking with Joseph

    Papi's Chili
    Cornbread
    Banana Pudding

- Epilogue
    Season everything with love and encouragement

简介

当我的儿子约瑟夫和我第一次想到一起做饭时，我不知道会成为这本书的催化剂。但是随着时间几个星期几个月的过去，我开始和我其他的孩子一起下厨，并且享受着和他们在厨房的每一分钟，这成为了我生活里面永远的习惯！每一次我会选择和我四个孩子其中的一个一起做饭。我们会很期待的在当天选择食谱，策划餐点，购买食材并一起烹饪。这是我所认为的和孩子在一起最特别的时候。有时候，你可能觉得这本书主要是写关于如何教育孩子的方法，但有时它其实看着却是一本关于食物和烹饪的书。因为我发现每一个人对爱和关注力都是一样的；只是每个人所对待的程度会不一样的问题。

"和爸爸一起下厨"是一本亲子关系与食谱结合的书籍。这是一本父母与孩子在许多层面上有关联的食谱。它包括了所有的"材料"以确保你的孩子知道他/她是被爱着和聆听着。虽然整本书的总体主题是烹饪，但烹饪并不是唯一的方法来找出孩子的自我，他们需要什么，以及我们如何找到最好的方法来确保他们能找到他们最有潜力的地方。这本书的主题其实是关于为什么我们要花时间在孩子身上，陪伴孩子。

我的一个朋友曾经说过教育孩子的秘诀就是"和他们坐在一起，直到他们18岁成年。"她的话并不是从字面上来说的这么简单，但其实意味着你花宝贵的时间越多的时间陪伴你的孩子，他们就会成为更好，更成功的人。这难道不是我们为人父母最想实现的吗？让他们成为每一个人都想接触的目标。

我发现，通过与我的孩子的烹饪和其他日常活动，我的花费是非常奇妙的，和孩子在一起的优质的时间不代表会打断你的日常活动。相反，有一些方法可以将其融入到实际中，使您的生活更轻松，现在和未来。为什么会更轻松呢？因为你会懂得你孩子的心情，并且你正在建立一种沟通习惯，一种一辈子的习惯。家里的其他人也将会学习如何切洋葱（努力工作）！

"和爸爸一起下厨"是为那些忙碌的单身妈妈们所写的，特别是那些在学校，工作和就寝时间之间寻找时间去陪伴孩子的妈妈。而对于那些爱孩子的爸爸们来说感觉就像他们在慢慢变老时，他们会失去了曾经和孩子所建立的密切关系。这是一本给天下父母的一本书。

与我们的孩子一起烹饪很重要，因为它能传授给父母和孩子非常多宝贵的课程。它教会了什么是团队合作，未雨绸缪，如何保持在材料预算范围内工作，一支竹子很容易折断，但几支竹在一起就很难折得断了。每个孩子都想成为一个喜欢制作美食的厨师吗？答案是不，当然不。但是，一些烹饪方式会吸引到每个孩子。一起挑选食谱的乐趣，去商店购买食材，掌握随时出现的困难，到最后看到一顿美好的膳食而作为大家幸苦努力的回报。更重要的是，通过烹饪，妈妈或爸爸可以把他们的时间和注意力专注在孩子身上。

作为一名教师和教育家，这本书探讨了我自己对儿童经验的每一个细节。前教育部长理查德·赖利曾经说过："我相信父母是孩子生活里第一任也是最重要的老师。"这句话我完全同意，因为教育孩子不仅仅是我们的责任，这也是我们的一种荣幸能够帮助他们成长和成熟，让他们有能力发掘这个世界上的奥秘。与你的孩子一起烹饪是日常生活里和孩子建立连接的一个奇妙的方式，当然这并不是唯一的方法。在本书里面我把我这么多年以来积累的方法和经验分享给每一位家长，而我自己的每一个孩子就是成功的证明。

在田纳西州举办的阅读专家会议上，在我发表这本书的主旨以及很多想法后，一位女士来到我的面前说，她最近和她十几岁的儿子一起做饭。

"噢，你有参加上一次的会议吗？"我问。

"不，但是我的一个朋友参加了，并且和我分享了这个想法，当时我对这个想法印象深刻，所以我就尝试了。"她说。

"那么，发生了什么事情呢？"我说。

"嗯，起初他以为我在开玩笑。他说："对，我不知道怎么样做饭，妈。"

"然后呢？"

"我说：不行，你可以帮我一起制作晚餐，我很想和你一起下厨，"然后从那时起，我们每次都在一起做饭。我觉得这是对我们来说最美好的事情。"她说。

我想这就是为什么我要写这本书的理由。所以，你就加入我们，与我和许多其他家长一起享受与我们自己的孩子一起的时光，沟通和乐趣。如果你真的很忙碌，你也可以撇开这本书，因为我们有"Quick Tips"和"Together！"列表可以让想法和活动一目了然。或者你可以阅读几个"Choose Your Sides"，以找到各人不同的方式，一个在您的家庭中常见的场景。但是，整本书充满了理想的原因还是在于为什么花时间与孩子一起度过是你家庭未来的最佳投资。

Introduction

When my son Joseph and I first thought of cooking together, I did not know it would become the catalyst for this book. But as the weeks and months went by, and I began cooking with my other children and loving every minute of it, it changed my life forever! I cook with one of my four children at a time. We look forward to choosing a recipe, planning meals, shopping and cooking on their day. It is our special time together. Sometimes this book is mostly tips on how to raise kids, and sometimes it seems like a book about food and cooking. I've found that the love and attention needed for either one are kind of the same; it is just a matter of degree.

"Cooking with Papi" is a connection cookbook. It is a recipe for connecting with your children on many levels. It has all the ingredients to insure your child knows he/she is loved and listened to. While the overarching theme is one of cooking, that is not the only way presented here to find out who your child is, what they need, and how to find the best way to make sure they reach their fullest, loving potential. This book is about taking time with your children.

A friend once said the secret to raising great kids was "sitting down on the floor with them until they're 18." She didn't mean that literally, but it does mean that the more really valuable time you spend with your kids, the better people they are going to be. And isn't that what we are trying to do as parents? Raise people other people want to be around?

I've found, through cooking with my children and other everyday activities, that spending marvelous, quality time with kids does not have to be an interruption to your day. Instead, there are ways to incorporate it to actually make your life easier, now and down the road. It will be easier because you will know your child's moods, you are setting up a lifelong habit of communication, and someone else in the house is going to learn how to chop onions!

"Cooking with My Papi" is written for the busy single Mom who is trying to find time with her kids between school, work and bedtime. It is for the Dad who loves his kids but feels like he is losing the close relationship he once had with them as they get older. It is for anyone that has children and has to feed them.

Cooking with our children is important because it teaches both parent and child so many lessons. It teaches teamwork, advanced planning, staying within a food budget, and that work isn't work when you can do it together. Does every child want to be a gourmet chef? No, of course not. But there are aspects of cooking together that will appeal to every child. It is the fun and power of helping choose recipes, going to the store to make sure you have the ingredients, being in charge of sharp objects, and seeing the reward of a wonderful meal to feed the family. And more than anything, it is Mom or Dad's devoted time and attention to just them.

As a teacher and educator, this book explores the rich details of my own experiences with children. Former Secretary of Education, Richard W. Riley once said, "I believe parents are the first and most important teachers in the lives of children." I completely agree and it is not just our responsibility to teach them well, it is our privilege to help them grow and mature and figure out the world. While cooking with your children is a marvelous way to connect on a daily basis, it is not the only way. I have included many other tips and activities I have developed over the years that have proven success in raising great kids.

After giving a keynote speech on many of the ideas in this book at a reading specialist conference in Tennessee, a woman came up to me and said that she had recently been cooking with her teenage son.

"Oh, did you attend a previous conference?" I asked.

"No, but a friend did and I was impressed with the idea, so I tried it," she said.

"So, how is it going?" I said.

"Well, at first he thought I was kidding. He said, 'Right, I don't know what to do, Mom.'"

"And then?"

"I said, 'No, you can help me out with dinner, I'd really like it.' And from then on, we cook all the time. It is the best thing that could have happened for us!" she said.

That is why I wrote the book. So, you can have the experiences, connection and fun with your children that I, and many, many others, have enjoyed with our own. You can skim the book if you are busy as there are **QuickTips** and **Together!** worksheets that have ideas and activities at a glance. Or you can read through a few **Choose Your Sides** to find different ways a common scene might be played out in your household. But the entire book is packed with terrific reasons why spending quality time with your children is the best investment in your family's future that you can make.

Communication

The recipe for connecting with your child

When my youngest child, Rianna, was little, my son Joseph had some friends over, just hanging out and playing. The boys were about 8 at the time. They were playing loudly and acting up and just being boys. Rianna had had enough. She hollered, "Would you guys stop, you're frustrating me?!"

Michael, my son's friend, started laughing and said, "How old is she?" She was two.

From the beginning, Rianna has been a great communicator and a little woman who knows her own mind. She knows what she needs and what she wants and I give credit to the hours we, (my wife Millie and I) have devoted to her language skills and simply listening to her. I have always thought it is best to give children, no matter how small, the tools and language we use. They will become as precise as we let them be. It might seem odd that a two-year-old would use the word

> **Quicktip**
>
> Watch for hints that your child has something to say. A kid that hangs around usually wants to talk. Don't make a big deal about it, just a simple, "Hey, what's up?" is usually enough to get things going.

"frustrating" but that is just what she was…frustrated! She might have also been annoyed, or borderline angry, but mostly she was frustrated, and she had the word to describe the feeling.

And more than that, she felt comfortable going in to a pack of big boys and telling them her feelings. *That* is communication. She needs, as all children do, to interact with the people in her family, verbally, every day. The simple act of speaking, talking, listening and learning can be done while you are picking them up from school or day care, helping them off with their boots, or getting ready for the family's dinner. You might be thinking, "Well, of course, I speak with my kids every day," but how is the in-depth listening, interacting and learning part going? Are you as sure as you can be that your child will continue talking to you into their tweens, teens and beyond? If we, as parents, take the time to truly listen to our children, the relationship grows deeps roots, strengthening the bond to us and the earth.

I like to use the Chinese character that means "To Listen" as a demonstration in my workshops.

You can see there are four elements:

1. Eye
2. Ears
3. Full Attention
4. Heart

Without beating yourself up, or planning on saving extra money for your child's therapy, think about how often you truly listen to your child with all four of these elements. Open your heart to hear what they are saying. Are there undercurrents? Is it really fear they are feeling and not just anger when they are beating up the sofa with their plastic bat? Do they have your full attention when they are telling you about the mean kid at day care again while you are driving and worrying about paying the phone bill and wondering if your Mom's surgery is serious? Listening, really listening, is a learned skill, and not many of us have learned it. It takes practice, but once learned, it is truly rewarding.

I understand that as parents we have nine billion things to do during the day. But few are more important than listening to our children. If we take the time to listen with our eyes, ears, full attention and most of all, heart, we are going to really build a relationship that will last a lifetime, even through the teen years. It will be a loving, positive relationship that will get both you and your child through anything.

What this positive communication is doing is helping your child think that the world is an okay place, and that they are okay in it. Research has found that we say 8,000 words to ourselves in one day. The shocking part is that 6,500 of them are negative! Whether it is how we were raised ourselves, or that the media says we aren't rich enough or thin enough or pretty enough, the reasons don't matter. The negative words just have to stop. And we have to make sure we don't pass this negative thinking on to the next generation. By being fair and consistent and loving in how we communicate, we are giving our children the most valuable tool ever, the ability to feel good about themselves.

So, how are we to go about this? How do we make sure that our children don't have 6,500 bad things to say about themselves every day? We do this by letting them know we are here, available, ready to listen. Is it always easy? Heck, no. To quote the character played by Tom Hanks in "A League of Their Own" it's "the hard that makes it great." I am not saying that listening or speaking with your child is hard, but sometimes finding the time to, is. Sometimes it is hard to listen to the reasons why they want their friends over when you are dead tired; our first reaction is again, heck, no. And it is hard to stop vacuuming when guests are coming over or to turn the television down when the game is on, but often, that is just what we need to do.

Here is an example.

Choose Your Sides

> *Your child just came up to you about the baby bunny he saw in the back yard and you know this is not going to be a short conversation because he loves baby bunnies and has been waiting all spring to see one. You are also on the phone with your best friend who is going through a terrible divorce. You...*

1. Tell your child bunnies grow up and die anyway so who cares.

2. Tell your friend "one moment please," and walk over to the window for a second, exclaim heartily and tell your child that "hurry, get a paper so you can draw it, and as soon as I am done speaking with Aunt Kathy, who is kind of upset, we can talk about it."

3. Tell your crying friend that it is a bunny emergency and you must go.

4. Tell your child absentmindedly, "great" and continue talking on the phone.

    I like number 2. But the key here is to really, really give them the attention this momentous occasion deserves once the phone call is done. This serves several purposes.

- It sets up trust in your child because you follow through with the very things you say you will do.

- It shows them that you care about what they care about.

- It also shows them that you will not drop everything you are doing immediately, every time they want something.

These are the things we come across EVERY DAY. And if every day we pay attention to these seeming little things, the big things take care of themselves.

I recently went on a picnic with my family. It felt so good to have everyone together sitting on a blanket enjoying the day together. There weren't squabbles or tantrums. We have four children, two boys and two girls ranging in age from 11 to 19. It hit me that our hard work is paying off! The hard work that starts at home and starts with us, as parents. I am developing healthy, happy, well-balanced children, who will be raising healthy, happy, well-balanced families of their own someday. By teaching our children to communicate well, they can easily speak with us, or their siblings or friends, about absolutely anything.

And by big things taking care of themselves, I mean your child's ability to handle speaking with someone when it is really important. They will be comfortable confiding in you about a scary encounter at the mall, a friend who wants to try drugs, wondering whether they should have sex with their boyfriend…and you thought baby bunnies' conversations were hard! Setting up a habit of daily communication that truly engages your children into thinking about their world and how they show up in it, gives back one-thousand fold down the line.

Here are some great ideas on connecting and communicating with your children.

Together!
- Accept the fact that you won't agree on everything. Never label a child's opinions, beliefs, feelings or experiences "childish," "silly," "funny," or "wrong."

- The fewer topics you declare "off limits," the more your kids will talk to you.

- If you don't know the answer to a question, help your kids find it.

- Be willing to talk in a place that is comfortable for your child. Don't insist that they "settle down" before you can talk.

- Ask your child's opinion or advice about something important.

- Have family dinners now and then where conversation focuses on one topic. Rotate whose turn it is to choose the subject.

- Ask your children every day about what they are doing and thinking. Tell them about your day, too. Form the habit of frequent conversation.

By incorporating these ideas into your daily life, your children are getting the key components needed to become great communicators. They will know that they are understood, that they are accepted and that their own ideas are Affirmed.

Communication Worksheet

Use this as you like. It can be a simple reference of things you want to do or copy it and hang it up somewhere as a reminder and check list of great communication tools!

Every day, I want to…

Tell my children "I love you"
Do at least one fun thing with them
Ask them how their day was
Tell them about my day
Look them in the eyes when I listen
Plan for our special time together that week
Imagine how they might feel about something, especially when they are upset
Notice when my child does well, and praise him/her for it

Together!

- 虽然家长肯定不会完全同意孩子所提出的观点。但是请不要给孩子的意见，信仰，感受或经历贴上"幼稚"，"愚蠢"，"有趣"或"错误"的标签。

- 减少你所"限制"的话题，你的孩子们就越会和你对话得更多。

- 如果你不知道问题的答案，请和你的孩子一起找到它。

- 只要是孩子觉得他们舒服和开心的地方我们都能和他们沟通。不要坚持说"安静下来"才跟你说话。

- 询问孩子对重要事项的意见或建议。

- 一家人坐在一起吃晚餐时，把谈话集中在一个话题上。然后开始再每人轮流提出一些有趣的话题一起讨论。

- 每天都向的孩子询问他们在做什么和思考什么。也告诉他们你在外面的一天过得怎么样。这就是养成勤于沟通的开始。

通过将以上这些想法融入到你的日常生活中，这样能使孩子成为一个出色的交流者。他们会知道他们的想法是被理解并珍视的，他们的想法是被接受的，他们自己的想法是被肯定的。

Communication Worksheet

如果你喜欢的话可以尝试一下将以下的话作为你每天必须和孩子做的一些小事情。可以是一些你想要做的事情的简单参考，并将其打印出来挂在某处，作为给自己的一个提醒。

每一天我都想。。。

告诉孩子"我爱你"
与他们至少做一件有趣的事情
问问他们今天如何
告诉他们我的一天发生了什么
当我听他们说话时，看着他们的眼睛
计划一下这周的特别时间一起去做些什么
想象一下他们对某件事情的感受如何，特别是当他们不高兴的时候
注意当孩子在任何事情上做得很好的时候一定要多点赞美他/她

Five Senses

Have your child label the flaps as follows: I See, I Hear, I taste, I Smell, I Touch. Ask your child to write and illustrate facts about each of the five senses inside. Or, he or she can list descriptive words under each flap such as sweet, spicy, sour, and salty under I Taste.

五感

让你的孩子标出如下皮瓣以这五种感觉：我看到，我听到，我尝到，我闻到，以及我摸到。请你的孩子写和说明这五种感官具体是什么。或者，他或她可以列出每个皮瓣下的描述性如：在我口味下它是甜，辣，酸或者咸。

Scratch n' Sniff Art

In advance, place assorted flavors of gelatin or powdered juice mix in separate bowls. Invite your child to sit at a table. Distribute a large piece of drawing paper to your child, and a pencil to draw a picture on their paper. Have your child lightly trace their picture with glue and sprinkle it with powdered juice mix or flavored gelatin. After the picture is dry, your child's picture may be scratched and sniffed

抓住嗅觉艺术

提前将各种口味的明胶或粉末汁混合在不同的碗中。然后让你的孩子坐在桌子旁边。给孩子一大块绘图纸并用铅笔在纸上画一张照片。让你的孩子轻轻地用胶水跟踪他们的照片,并将果汁混合物或调味的明胶撒上。等图片干后,你的小孩就可以触摸的触感并嗅出图片的味道。

Textured Names

In advance, collect several textured materials (e.g. seeds, pasta, beans, cotton, cereal, pompoms, buttons) and place them in separate containers. Place the containers, cardboard, markers and glue on a table. Invite family members to sit at the table and use a marker to print their name in large print on a piece of cardboard. Have family members trace their name with glue and cover each letter with a textured material. Allow time for the glue to dry. Then have them close their eyes and use their sense of touch to "read" each other's names.

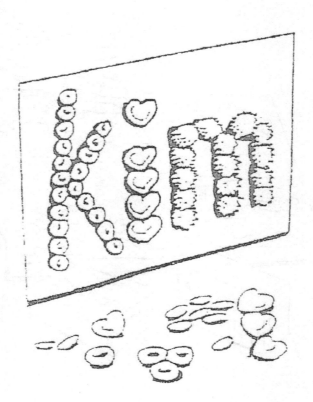

每种纹理的名称

提前收集几种纹理材料（例如种子，面食，豆类，棉花，谷物，肥皂，钮扣）并将每种材料单独放在分开的容器中。将容器，纸板，标记物和胶水放在桌子上。邀请家人坐在桌子旁边，用一个标记在一块纸板上大幅印刷他们的名字。让家人用胶水写出他们的名字，并用纹理材料覆盖每封信。 让胶水干燥时间。然后让他们闭上眼睛，用自己的触觉来"读"彼此的名字

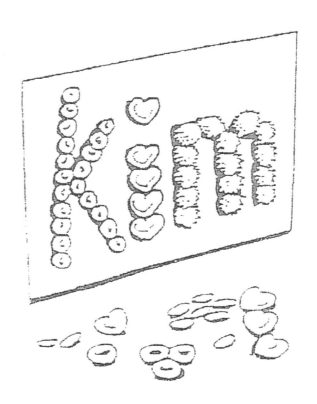

Cooking with Rianna

Spending time with your children is more important than spending money on your children

Refried Beans

Ingredients:

- 1 ½ lbs. of pinto beans
- 1 whole medium onion
- ½ medium chopped onion
- Salt to taste
- 2 tablespoons canola oil

Directions:

Boiling Beans:

- Clean and rinse beans

- Place beans in a large pot and fill with water 2 inches below the top

- Add one whole peeled onion and salt and bring to a boil. After bringing to a boil reduce heat to low.

- Cook beans for 2-2 1/2 hours stirring occasionally until beans are soft

Refrying Beans:

- Place cooked beans with juice in blender and blend until smooth

- In a large skillet sauté ½ chopped onion in 2 tablespoons of oil

- Pour blended beans in medium skillet of sautéed onion. Heat with onions for 10 minutes stirring constantly

Spanish Rice

Ingredients:

- 2 cups long grain rice
- ½ medium onion
- 1 whole clove garlic minced
- 1 8 oz. can tomato juice
- 2 tablespoons canola oil
- 3 cups warm water
- Salt to taste
- Pepper to taste

Directions:

- In a large skillet, sauté onions and garlic in oil
- Add rice to sautéed onions and garlic for 3-4 minutes stirring constantly
- Add tomato juice and warm water
- Salt and pepper to taste
- Lower heat to simmer, cover skillet and cook for 20 minutes

Green Chile and Pork

Ingredients:

- 1 18 oz. can tomato juice
- 1 lb. pork shoulder
- 12 Anaheim Peppers
- 1 tablespoons Lawry's seasoning
- 1 tablespoons salt
- 1 tablespoon pepper
- 1 whole onion

Directions:

- Place pork shoulder in a large pot and add water. Add a whole onion, salt and pepper

- Boil until pork falls apart and remove from pot and shred

- Preheat oven to 500° F. Place the Anaheim peppers in one layer on a baking sheet and place in the oven. Roast the peppers, turning them occasionally, until the skin is blistered on all sides and starting to turn black, about 15-20 minutes. Remove the peppers from oven and place in a large bowl, cover with a lid or plastic wrap and set aside to cool

- Carefully remove the skins from the peppers with your fingers. Cut a slit down the side of each pepper and carefully remove any seeds and white membrane.

- In a large pot combine pork, peppers, seasoning, salt, black pepper and tomato juice

- Heat on medium flame for 20 minutes stirring occasionally
- Serve with refried beans and Spanish rice

Tortilla Treats

Ingredients:

- 4 medium flour tortillas
- 1-12 oz. package of chocolate chips
- 1 bottle caramel syrup
- ½ cup chopped almonds

Directions:

- Pre-heat oven to 425° F

- Cut each tortilla into 8 equal triangles

- Place triangles on a cookie sheet and bake for 8 minutes

- Let baked tortilla cool for 15 minutes

- Using a double boiler melt the package of chocolate chips

- Spread melted chocolate on top of each baked triangle

- Let chocolate cool for a few minutes

- Drizzle caramel sundae syrup on top of the chocolate covered tortilla triangle

- Sprinkle chopped almonds on top of triangle

- Place in refrigerator for 15 minutes to cool before serving

Planning and Decision Making

Make list, buy ingredients, reap rewards

At first glance, if might not seem like Planning and Decision Making belong in the same chapter. But what I have found in my years of education and helping families is that unless a child learns how to plan, his/her decisions are tougher to make. Planning and decision making go hand-in-hand. Planning ahead for things can help the decision-making process. Every day we have choices to make; so, do our children. Planning for things that they want, making a homework plan, which shows to watch on TV involves both planning and decision making.

Planning leads to success. Giving our children little choices and decisions, they can make when they are young, will insure they will be successful decision makers as they get older. We can start as early as two or three years old with a trip for back to pre-school clothes. Watch your child calm down in the store when you get them actively involved in the process of buying their clothes. The choices at this age will be guided by you, but ultimately chosen by them. For instance, we are not going to let our little girl have free rein in the junior department so she decides to get the hootchy midriff tops, but we can choose a few appropriate shirts and ask, "Do you want the pink shirt or the orange?"

When my son James was just three years old, those light-up shoes were in fashion. Both James and Joseph needed new tennis shoes, but only James wanted the light-up kind. My wife, Millie, and I were afraid James would tire of them, or that they would be annoying to the rest of us and the world by lighting up all the time. We were wrong and James was right. He insisted, at three years of age, that those were the shoes for him. He did not throw a tantrum but just insisted that they were the best shoes in the world. James enjoyed those shoes for months and months, until he outgrew them.

He showed complete strangers his shoes, pointed out the lights, and mentioned the fact that he had chosen them himself. He delighted in surprising unsuspecting people with his shoes flash and dash. He walked proud and happy. And we, his family, delighted in seeing him that way. He made the decision and was thrilled with it.

Allowing children to make choices is an everyday occurrence, an everyday strategy that empowers them.

Some of the worst times of our own lives are when we felt we had no control over our surroundings or that decisions were too often made for us instead of making our own. By giving your children some control over their environment and some of the happenings in their world, you are encouraging them to be confident kids and adults.

Before we get too far into helping children plan and make decisions, I want to use an example which demonstrates how the two intertwine. Let us say you have your high school reunion coming up in a few days. There is absolutely nothing in your closet you want to wear so you go shopping with friends. (As an example, we are using a mom, feel free to substitute "suit" for dress for the dads) Anyway, there it is, you see a beautiful red dress, you try it on and you look really, really good in it…it is also way over your budget. You don't get paid until Monday, the reunion is this Saturday and you do not want to let it go. What are your options?

- You can borrow money from one of your friends, and you can come up with a plan to pay them back
- Perhaps you will charge it and make sure to pay it off at the end of the month

- There are still a few days so you could put it on hold, take another look in your closet and see if you truly do not have anything that looks as good as that hot red dress

So, what is your plan? Have you made a decision yet? You might feel guilty asking your friend for money, or it might be the best idea. Your charge card might be maxed out or perhaps you just paid it all off and do not feel badly putting this one special purchase on it. Maybe no one has seen you in that dress you got for your cousin's wedding in the summer and you now remembered how many compliments you got on it. Thinking about your choices, are the rewards worth the sacrifice? After weighing these options, you come up with a plan and you can now make a decision.

Look at everything that goes in this seemingly simple decision of whether or not you should buy a new outfit. But it isn't really all that simple as there are always pros and cons. Planning and decision making involves looking at many of our choices, deciding which is best, and planning accordingly. The power we have as parents to guide our children to handle some of life's decisions can not start too early. Do we want them to start making decisions in high school when it is whether or not to drink with friends or skip school? Didn't think so.

The wonderful thing about teaching children early about making good decisions is that it is a skill that once learned, is never unlearned. Also, it grows and matures as they do, helping them see the advantages, and disadvantages, of certain decisions and risk-taking. A friend of mine usually ends his conversations with his 15 and 21-year old sons with "make good decisions." After he says, "I love you" he signs off by saying "Bye, Son, make good decisions." Once we learn how to make good decisions, isn't everything else pretty easy?

Attitude

With planning, often the hardest part with children is the right attitude. Anything, even a trip to the dentist or getting ice cream, can be improved or made miserable depending on attitude. If children look forward to something, the planning will go seamlessly. If they are dreading a long assignment, perhaps the last thing they want to do is plan for it. To them, it is easier to ignore it until the last minute.

One thing we need to teach our children is that not making a decision is actually just the opposite. When we don't make a decision, we are putting that decision into the hands and minds of others. If a decision has to be made, it might as well be made by them. Planning for things, making decisions, having the right attitude, is about choices.

Here is a great quote about attitude by NFL coach Vince Lombardi...

> The longer I live, the more I realize the impact of attitudes on life. Attitudes, to me, are more important than fact. It is more important than the past, than education, than money, than circumstances, than failures, than successes, than what other people say or think or do. It is more important than appearance, giftedness, or skill.
>
> It will make or break a company...a church...a home. The remarkable thing is we have a choice every day regarding the attitude we will embrace for that day. We cannot change our past...we cannot change the fact that people will act in a certain way. We cannot change the inevitable. The only thing we can do is play on the one string we have, and that is our attitude...I am convinced that life is

10% what happens to me, and 90% how I react to it. And so, it is with you…We are in charge of our attitudes."

Vince Lombardi

Hasn't there been something you did not want to do, but once you got rid of your negativity and wanting it to be over before it started, it wasn't that bad. We don't have to pretend that everything is terrific, (I never liked doing really long papers in school either), but we need to be models for our children how a positive attitude improves just about everything. Some ways to improve outlook, attitude and planning are…

- Help them see that putting things off just makes the now worse (by dreading it) and the later worse (because it isn't done yet)
- Use positive words and phrases instead of negative. Keep things light.
    - Avoid letting them use "hate." "I know you don't like cleaning your room as much as having friends over, but you really can't have one without the other…they would get lost!"
- Putting them in charge of when they will plan and make decisions can help them feel in charge and will improve attitude.

- "We have to set a schedule for homework, your project, and baseball by Thursday; when do you want to do it?"

Letting children know that they are in partnership with you in helping them plan, makes them feel more in control and less dreadful, of things they would rather not do and behavior in general. My workshops take lots of planning, organization and decision-making. The most fun part is the actual teaching and interacting with parents, but it is the hard work I put in ahead of time that lets me feel confident to bring the best experience possible to everyone, including me.

Planning a Homework Space

One of the best ways to involve your child in planning and decision-making is to talk about setting up their own spot to do homework. We often forget that we like a good place to pay our bills, do at home office work or just sit and surf on the computer that we know is ours. Children need this even more as it is difficult enough to get them to be enthusiastic about doing their homework.

But if we give them the chance to choose where in the house they can set up their little homework shop, and that it is ready for them when they need it, many things have happened. Your child will feel like she has had a say in this location, they know where to do their work, and it is ready for them without clearing off a table, sitting in front of the television or fighting for space with a brother or sister. This type of planning leads to successful homework nights.

Do you have a social child that can work in a room full of people and still get it done? Or is your son or daughter easily distracted or bothered by noise when trying to concentrate. Help them think through this Homework Space idea and plan accordingly. I am not talking about adding a room to the house and buying a new high-end desk and filing cabinet. A space for homework can be a corner of the living room that has a small table and chair, pens and erasers, and a few personal items that are the children's. Perhaps one child wants to do homework as you cook and likes to sit on the floor on his favorite homework rug. The important thing is to get them thinking about it and opening up some dialogue.

Mom or Dad, "I was thinking that you don't have a really nice place to do homework that is just yours. Where do you think a good place would be?" It should be quiet, only theirs unless they want to share, and not used for too many other things. Their favorite chair in front of the television can be problematic when it is usually a place for entertainment. A Homework Space means business and they will usually settle in and get to work much more quickly and easily.

Here are some things to think about when helping a child choose a Homework Space:

Together!

- Would you like to be around other people or do you want your space to be fairly quiet?
- This corner of the dining room is great! Do you want some decals or decorations around your table?
- I appreciate that you want to do homework in your room, but in the past we thought there were too many distractions and it took you a very long time to get it done. I don't like to see you so frustrated. Do you want to try it one more time or would you

like to set up a place out here where I can help you stay on task?

Planning a homework space might take a Family Meeting if there are one or more of your family members that will need their own space. Family Meetings are the ultimate planning tool for letting everyone in on big or small decisions that affect them. It will show your child that their private space is important to get work done easily and that you value their decision. Setting aside time for family meetings is a surefire way to get decisions made quickly.

Family Meetings
1. Make sure everyone can see each other. Sit in a circle on the floor or around a table.
2. Negativity is not allowed. All ages, ideas and discussion are welcome.
3. Make a list of what needs to be accomplished and try to stick to it.
4. Praise good ideas and teamwork.
5. End the meeting with what has been accomplished, who is to do what, and what needs to be discussed at a later

meeting. This avoids surprises and "But I didn't know I was supposed to!!"

Often in our hurried world a family meeting lets everyone know they are valued more than work, play or friends. Even children and teens most reluctant to join, will come back later with fond memories of "I thought they were dumb at the time, but I knew my Mom and Dad were really listening to me." You will be surprised at how your children can work together, with you and each other, to find solutions to problems of homework space, scheduling conflicts and time management. Kids are smart, and getting smarter all the time. If we allow our children to develop their own concepts of what they need, like and can do, our jobs just become easier.

> **Planning Quick Tips**
>
> 1. Have family meetings to talk about plans that affect the whole family.
>
> 2. Prompt good planning by asking questions, but don't take over the process.
>
> 3. Allow for mistakes. Don't blow up at a poor choice, but don't rescue your child from the consequences.
>
> 4. Point out to your children that not making a choice *is* making a choice – it's choosing not to choose. Explain that this gives someone else the power to determine what happens next.
>
> *From "What Kids Need to Succeed", by Peter L. Benson Judy Galbraith and Pamela Espeland*

一起！

- 你想要有别人在身边，还是想让你周围的空间非常安静？
- 饭厅的这个角落很棒！你想在桌子周围放一些贴花或装饰品吗？
- 我知道你想在你的房间做功课，但是我们认为这样你会分心，需要花更长时间才能完成。我不喜欢看到你因此而沮丧。你还是想去房间里面做还是想在这里设置一个地方，这样我可以更好的帮助你。

规划一个做作业的地方可能需要和家人之间商量一下因为如果有一个或多个家庭成员需要自己的空间而导致空间不够用的问题。会议是最有用的规划工具，因为这样让每个人都能够参与并讨论对影响他们的大或小的决策。这样的意义是会让你的孩子了解到专业空间的重要性，以便轻松完成的工作，以及让他们知道你重视他们的决定。家庭聚会的时间是快速做出决定的一个肯定的方式。

家庭会议

1. 确保每个人都能互相看到对方。可以坐在地板上或桌子周围的一个圆圈。
2. 不允许消极。欢迎所有年龄，想法并一起参与讨论。
3. 列出需要完成的工作，并尝试坚持下去。
4. 赞美好的想法和团队精神。
5. 结束会议，要总结会上做了什么，谁做了什么，还有什么需要在以后的会议上讨论。这避免了"我不知道我应该做什么是！"的情况发生。

通常在我们匆忙的世界里，一个小小的家庭会议让每个家庭成员都知道他们在我们心中的地位比工作，玩乐或朋友更加重。即使是最不愿意加入的孩子和青少年，也会在以后的回忆中："我以为他们当时的做法很笨，但是我知道我的妈妈和爸爸真的有在聆听我的话"。你会惊讶于你的每一个孩子是如何团结在一起干活，与家长或者彼此的同龄人，例如找到方法解决作业空间的问题，日程表冲突问题和最重要的时间管理。孩子们很聪明，他们一直都在变得更聪明。如果我们允许我们的孩子们发展一套属于自己的观念，让他们了解到他们所需要的，喜欢的和能做的，我们的工作就变得更容易了。

Taming the Tube/Computer/Phone/iPad etc.

This is one of the biggest things in child-raising today and is a great topic for a Family Meeting. The days of kids running around outside on bikes from dawn to dusk are gone. There are safety issues, but more than that, there are technology issues. Here are some frightening statistics on television use alone...

- Hours per day that TV is on in an average U.S. home:
    - *7 hours and 12 minutes*
- Number of minutes per week that parents spend in meaningful conversation with their children:
    - *38.5 minutes*
- Number of minutes per week that the average American child ages 2-11 watches TV:
    - *1,197 minutes (about 20 hours)*
- Hours per week of TV watching shown to negatively affect academic achievement:
    - *10 or more hours*
- Percentage of 4th graders who watch more than 14 hours of television per week:
    - *81%*

- Percent of children polled who said they felt "upset" or "scared" by violence on television:
    - *91%*

Also, children, particularly when they are young, have a hard time telling the difference between real people and scenarios and what they see on television or video games. Computers and television can be great tools, or complete time wasters. Technology has given us the means to connect with people, or to cut them off, depending on how it is used. How do you want your family to use technology? Think about some of these questions and decide what will work for your family.

- What is a good age for a child to get a cell phone? How will it be used? What are the limits?
- Television should not be watched while doing homework. How about the computer if it is not necessary for the assignment?
- Let the children discuss the parents' technology use…are you using the phone or computer or television too much? Be prepared for honest answers.

- Setting time limits and consequences should be agreed upon. Reading, playing outside, exercising, or playing board games all stimulate the mind and body better than mindless television watching.
- Be a positive role model and let the kids give you consequences if you are on the phone for three hours one day gossiping with your sister. It doesn't have to be much, but they can see that life can be fair once in a while.
- Try log sheets if family members are having a hard time keeping track of their hours spent using the computer, etc. I wouldn't encourage spying, but let everyone know that they must be accurate.

Communicating is done all the time with computers and televisions around. But it may not be the interactive, loving kind of communication that lets your children know what is important. Make sure they know that technology is terrific and that any limits all of you decide as a family are meant to get your family to be the smartest, brightest, most connected family around!

Techno Log Sheet				
Name	Date	TV	Computer	Phone
Susie		3-4:30		
Jamal				
Mom				
Dad				

You can copy this page and use for your own family.

Techno Log Sheet				
Name	Date	TV	Computer	Phone

1- Have family meetings to talk about plans that affect the whole family. Invite suggestions from everyone, even the youngest children.

2- Give your teenager full responsibility for planning and preparing a family meal once a month.

3- Model planning and decision making. Have things-to-do lists and calendars visible in your home. Give your children daily planners or date books and demonstrate how to use them.

4- When your children receive long-term assignments, offer to help them plan and make decisions in order to finish on time.

5- Give your teenager increasing responsibility for planning his or her own future.

Examples: saving money for a special purchase; finding a summer job. Prompt good planning by asking questions, but don't take over the planning process.

6- Model choice making: 1) gathering information, 2) viewing the choice from all sides, 3) weighing potential consequences, 4) listing pros and cons, 5) making a choice and sticking to it. Help your children apply this process to choices they're facing.

7- Talk your children through choices. Use "what if?" questions to help them anticipate consequences. *Example:* "What if you don't clean your room by Friday when your friend comes to spend the night?"

8- Allow for mistakes. Don't blow up at a poor choice, and don't rescue your child from the consequences.

9- Encourage your kids to keep a journal of the choices they make. Explain that they should write down what happened *and* how they felt at the time. This reinforces good choices and serves as a strong reminder of the effects of bad choices.

10- Point out to your children that not making a choice *is* making a choice – it's choosing not to choose. Explain that this gives someone else the power to determine what happens next.

1. 举行家庭会议谈论影响全家的计划。邀请每个人，甚至最小的孩子也可以提出建议。
2. 给处于青少年阶段的孩子负责规划和亲手准备一个月一次的家庭餐。
3. 示范规划与决策。在家中可以放一个每日要做的小列表。给你的孩子制作每日规划或日期书，并演示如何使用它们。
4. 当您的孩子被分配长期任务时，给他们提供帮助让他们计划和作出决定以及时完成所要求的任务。
5. 让处于青少年阶段的孩子学会负责规划自己的未来。

    示例：金钱要花在该花的地方；找暑期工。给他们提出好的规划建议，但不要接管规划过程。
6. 模式选择：1）收集信息 2）查看各方的选择 3）称量潜在后果 4）列出优缺点 5）作出选择并坚持。帮助你的孩子将这个过程应用到他们所面临的选择上。

7. 通过选择来谈谈你的孩子。使用"如果？"问题来帮助他们预测后果。例如："如果星期五晚上你朋友来过夜但是你没有事前打扫房间会怎么办？"

8. 允许犯错误。不要在不好的选择中发脾气，也不要从后果里拯救你的孩子，因为他们要知道每一个抉择都要承担其所带来的后果。

9. 鼓励你的孩子记录下来他们所做的每一个选择。要他们记下当时发生的事情和感受。这加强了良好的选择，并强烈提醒了不良选择所带来的影响。

10. 让孩子知道没有选择也是在做出选择 - 选择不去选择。这也就说明了让别人有权力确定接下来会发生什么。

Television

To make a T.V. sack, glue a piece of white paper on the front of a brown sack. Draw or glue on construction paper, for On and Off knobs. Have your child make a sack television, write or draw picture activities they can do instead of watching T.V. and place them in their Television sack. Have your child pull an activity out of the sack and do it together

电视

制作 T.V.袋子,在一个棕色的袋子的前面粘一张白纸。在建筑纸上绘制或胶合一个用于开和关旋钮。让你的孩子自己做一个"麻袋电视",写出或画出他们可以做的图片活动,而不是看单纯的看电视,并把图片放在他们的电视袋里面。然后让你的孩子从袋子里拉出一个他们想做的活动并和他们一起做。

Character, Setting, Problem and Solution

Read a book with your child that has a problem and a solution. Then ask your child to record the main characters, the setting, the problem and the solution for the story they have read.

角色，设定，问题和解决方案

与孩子一起阅读一本包括问题和解决方法的书。然后请你的孩子记录他们读过的故事的主要角色，设定，问题和解决方案。

Riddle Box

Have your child place a picture or object inside a box. Show your child how to cut and blue on paper to fit the lid and ask your child to write a riddle about what is in the box.

谜语盒

让孩子将一张图片或物品放在一个盒子里面。告诉你的孩子如何裁纸和粘贴以适应盖子的大小，并要求你的孩子写一个谜语放在盒子里。

Cooking with Raquel

To the world you may just be one person, but to one person you may just be the world

Wonton Salad

Ingredients:

- 5 boneless and skinless chicken breasts
- 1 package Wonton skins, cut in strips and deep fried
- 1 head of lettuce (Chopped)
- 1 bunch green onions (Chopped)
- ¼ cup slivered almonds
- ½ cup canola oil

Sauce:

- ¼ cup vinegar
- ¼ cup catsup
- ¼ water
- 6 tablespoons sugar
- 1 tablespoon soy sauce
- 1 tablespoon cornstarch
- 2 tablespoons water

Directions:

- Boil chicken in water adding salt and pepper and whole onion

- After chicken is cooked, take out of water and shred

- Cut wonton skin in strips

- In medium skillet fry wontons and place on paper towel to drain

Sauce:

- Combine vinegar, catsup, water, sugar and soy sauce and bring to a boil stirring constantly.

- Mix 2 tablespoons of cornstarch and water in a small bowl making sure mixture is without lumps.

- Add cornstarch to mixture and cook constantly stirring until mixture thickens

- Combine all ingredients in a salad bowl then add sauce to taste

Chicken Avocado Egg Rolls

Ingredients:

2 tablespoons canola oil
¼ cup finely minced red bell peppers
1 tablespoon minced garlic
¼ cup finely chopped celery
2 cups shredded chicken breast
½ cup shredded carrots
12 egg roll wrappers into 24 pieces
1 egg

½ cup finely minced red onion
2 tablespoons minced ginger
¼ cup slide bamboo shoots
¼ cup soy sauce
1 cup julienned green cabbage
4 cups canola oil
2 avocados, sliced
1 tablespoon milk

Directions:

- Heat canola over high heat. Sauté red onions and bell peppers until translucent.

- Add ginger, garlic, bamboo shoots, celery, chicken, and cook for 5 minutes over medium heat.

- Deglaze pan with soy sauce. Cool mixture.

- In large bowl combine cabbage, carrots and chicken mixture.

- In medium saucepan, heat oil to 350° F.

- Oil needs to be deep enough to keep egg roll from touching bottom of pan

- To roll egg rolls, layout egg roll skin with corner facing you, place approximately 1/12th of mixture on roll and place 2 pieces of avocado on top of mixture.

- Fold corner over mixture, and then fold outside corners over the mixture, making a roll, 4 to 5-inches wide.

- Roll firmly, being careful not to tear wrapper, and seal the final edge with egg wash.

- Dredge the egg roll in egg wash, allow excess to drain off and submerge egg roll in oil.

- Fry until golden brown, about 3 to 4 minutes.

- Drain on sheet tray lined with a cooling rack

Wonton Treats

Ingredients:

- 1 package Wonton skins
- 2 cups Canola Oil
- ¼ cup sugar
- 2 tablespoons Cinnamon

Directions:

- Heat oil in small skillet
- While oil is heating, combine sugar and cinnamon
- Fry wontons until golden brown
- Remove wonton from oil and sprinkle with sugar/cinnamon
- Serve and Enjoy

Cooking with James

Every father should remember that one day his son will follow his example instead of his advice

Fried Rice

Ingredients:

- 2 green onions
- 2 large eggs
- 1 teaspoon salt
- Pepper to taste
- 4 tablespoons oil for stir-frying
- 4 cups cold cooked rice
- 1-2 tablespoons light soy sauce as desired
- 1 small can of mixed vegetables

Directions:

- Wash and finely chop green onion
- Lightly beat eggs with salt and pepper
- Add 2 tablespoons to heated wok or frying pan
- Add eggs to hot oil
- Cook, stirring until they are lightly scrambled but not dry
- Remove eggs and clean out pan
- Add 2 tablespoons oil to cleaned pan and heat

- Add rice and stir-fry for a few minutes using a wooden spoon to break it apart
- Stir in soy sauce
- When rice is heated through, add scrambled eggs , green onion and mixed vegetables

炒饭

- 配料：
- •2 个洋葱
- •2 个鸡蛋
- •1 茶匙盐
- •胡椒粉适量
- •4 汤匙油煎炒
- •4 杯冷饭
- •1-2 汤匙轻质酱油
- •1 些混合类型蔬菜

- 做法：
- •洗净并切碎葱
- •用盐和胡椒给鸡蛋调味
- •加入 2 汤匙油加热炒锅
- •将鸡蛋加入热油中
- •翻炒并搅拌至轻度搅拌但不全熟
- •取出炒鸡蛋并清理锅
- •加 2 汤匙油清洗锅和加热

- •用木勺将米饭炒几分钟,将其每粒分开
- •加入酱油继续翻炒
- •当米饭炒热时,加入炒鸡蛋和混合蔬菜过两分钟然后起锅

Vegetable Chow Mein

Ingredients:
- ½ LB fresh egg noodles (3 oz. dried)
- ½ cup yellow onion (thinly sliced)
- 1 cup bell pepper (red, thinly sliced)
- 1 zucchini (cut into thin strips)
- 1 cup mushrooms (thinly sliced
- 1 tablespoon fresh ginger (grated)
- 2 cloves garlic (minced)
- 4 tablespoons oil

For the Sauce:
- 2 tablespoons oyster sauce
- 2 tablespoons soy sauce
- 1 tablespoon light soy sauce
- 2 tablespoons rice vinegar
- 1 teaspoon sesame oil (toasted)

Directions:

- Bring a large pot of water to a boil and add 1 tablespoon of salt. Boil the noodles for 2 minutes, drain and rinse well with cold water.
- Place the noodles in bowl and toss with 1 tablespoon of oil.
- In a small bowl, combine the sauce ingredients with 3 tablespoons of water and set aside
- Heat a large non-stick pan until very hot. Add 2 tablespoons of oil and sauté the onion and red bell pepper until just tender, about 2 minutes
- Add zucchini and mushrooms and continue to stir-fry until golden brown, about 5 minutes. Transfer the vegetables to a bowl.
- Reheat the same pan until very hot. Add remaining 2 tablespoons of oil and sauté ginger and garlic for several seconds. Add noodles and stir-fry until the noodles are heated, about 5 minutes
- Add vegetables to the pan with the noodles and add the sauce and toss until well combined and heated.

蔬菜炒面

配料：

- 半磅鲜鸡蛋面（3盎司干面）
- 半杯黄葱（薄切片）
- 1杯甜椒（红，薄切）
- 1个西葫芦（切成薄条）
- 1杯蘑菇（薄切片）
- 1茶匙鲜姜（磨碎）
- 2瓣大蒜（切碎）
- 4汤匙油

酱汁：

- 2汤匙蚝油
- 2汤匙酱油
- 1汤匙轻质酱油
- 2汤匙米醋
- 1茶匙芝麻油（烤）

做法：

- 开锅烧水，加入1汤匙盐。煮面条2分钟，用冷水冲洗干净。
- 将面条放入碗中，用1汤匙油搅拌。
- 在一个小碗中，将所有酱料与3汤匙水混合在一起
- 烧红不粘锅。加入2汤匙油，炒洋葱和红椒胡椒，直到断生，约2分钟
- 加入西葫芦和蘑菇，继续搅拌至金黄色约5分钟。将蔬菜捞处到碗里。
- 重新加热锅。加入剩余的2汤匙油，炒香姜和蒜。然后加入面条炒，直至面条熟透，约5分钟。
- 用面条将蔬菜加入锅中，加入酱汁，并加热搅拌均匀。

Orange Pork Chop Stir-Fry

Ingredients:
- 4 Boneless pork chops (about 1 ½ pounds)
- For Marinade:
- 1 tablespoon rice wine or dry sherry
- 2 teaspoons cornstarch

For Sauce:
- 1/3 cup orange juice
- 2 tablespoons water
- 2 tablespoons soy sauce
- 1 ½ teaspoons liquid honey

Other:
- 2 slices ginger (chopped)
- 1 Garlic clove (Chopped)
- 2 Baby bok choy
- ½ cup baby carrots
- 2 teaspoons cornstarch mixed in
- 4 teaspoons water
- A few drops sesame oil as needed
- 4 tablespoons oil for stir-frying as needed

Directions:

- Rinse pork chops, pat dry and cut into cubes. Add rice wine and cornstarch and marinate for 30 minutes.

- While the pork is marinating prepare the vegetables and sauce. Wash the baby bok choy, drain, and chop separating the leaves and stalks. Wash and drain the baby carrots and cut in half. Combine the cornstarch and water in a small bowl and set aside.

- Add 2 tablespoons of oil to a heated wok or frying pan. When the oil is hot add pork chops cubes. Let the pork chops cook for a minute and then stir0fry until they change color and are nearly cooked. Remove from wok and drain on paper towels.

- Clean out the wok and add more oil. Add garlic and ginger when oil is very hot. Stir-fry briefly until aromatic. Add carrots and stir-fry briefly. Add bok choy stalks and leave and stir-fry until they turn bright green.

- Make a well in the middle of the wok and add the sauce. Turn up the heat and give the cornstarch and water mixture a quick re-sir and add it to the sauce, stirring quickly to thicken.

- Add a few drops of sesame oil and serve hot with cooked rice.

橙汁猪排

配料：

- 4个无骨猪排（约 1½磅）

- 腌料：
- 1汤匙米酒或干雪利酒
- 2茶匙玉米淀粉

调料：
- 1/3 杯橙汁
- 2汤匙水
- 2汤匙酱油
- 1½茶匙液体蜂蜜

其他：
- 2片姜（切碎）
- 1大蒜丁香（切碎）
- 2个小白菜
- ½杯小胡萝卜

- 2茶匙玉米淀粉混合
- 4茶匙水
- 根据需要滴几滴芝麻油
- 4汤匙油,根据需要进行炒锅

做法:
- 冲洗猪排,擦干,切成块。加入米酒和玉米淀粉腌30分钟。
- 猪肉腌制准备蔬菜和酱汁。洗净白菜,沥干水,切菜。洗净小胡萝卜并切成两半。将玉米淀粉和水合并在一个小碗中,放在一边。
- 将2汤匙油加入已经热锅中。当油热时加入猪排。让猪排煮一分钟,然后搅拌,直到变色,大概八成熟。从锅中取出并用纸巾抽走多余油脂。
- 清理油锅并放入油。当油滚时加入大蒜和姜。短暂翻炒出香味。放入胡萝卜。再加上切好的白菜一起翻炒直至翠绿。
- 在锅的中间一个点加入酱汁并加热,将玉米淀粉和水混合物快速重新加入酱中,快速搅拌加稠。

•加入几滴芝麻油,将酱料淋在猪排上,配上一碗米饭,这样就完美了。

Boundaries and Discipline

Without rules, there is baking chaos

There is a very good reason the human baby is cute. They cause their parents sleepless nights and frustration with unknown demands, crying and chaos. If they weren't so cute and lovable, we might not keep them. Children stay cute for a long time, and by then we love them so much it is hard to refuse them anything. When your child is looking up at you with those big brown or blue or green eyes, pleading innocently, it is tough to say no. By setting up boundaries and their knowing consequences ahead of time, children will pester less often and thus, be more content.

Knowing ahead of time what is expected, for both parents and children, makes life much easier. It takes away the negative connotations associated with learning rules and sticking to them. There are several things I want to talk about in this chapter but really, they come under two major headings:

- Respect: earning it and giving it

    o "First, do no harm"

- Family guidelines: learning them and keeping them
    - It's hard to play the game if you don't know the rules

Respecting a family's boundaries is a carryover from showing respect by both parents and children. We cannot demand our children to respect us if we do not earn it by being consistent, purposeful parents. And children will not respect boundaries set for them if they are not valid, known and discussed ahead of time.

Yelling, screaming, hitting and belittling are not only dangerous, possibly illegal and sad, they just don't work. By knowing a few gentle tools for discipline that really work, your family will be calmer and happier. Think of the tools I give you in this chapter as part of a toolbox. Use whichever ones work for your family. Your family might not need all of them. Stay interested, change things when needed and err on the side of calm.

If asked, many parents don't think of the word "respect" in relation to their children but it is exactly what we need to think about. Respect means to "show regard or consideration for… esteem for or the sense of worth or excellence of a person." We have this exercise in our workshops that gets amazing results every time. We have the parents do it around the third week of the course so everyone knows each other and they are comfortable sharing. You can do it as well; it truly has a huge impact and it deals directly with respect and esteem.

尊重家庭规矩是家长和孩子互相尊重的传承。如果我们作为家长每天只顾着在外面拼搏挣钱而忽视掉给孩子的陪伴，这样我们不能要求我们的孩子尊重我们。如果不能有效地提前和儿童互相了解和讨论，儿童不会尊重我们为他们设定的界限。

大喊大叫，打击和贬低不单单是危险的行为，而且可能触犯法律和造成悲伤的后果，这些行为是行不通的。通过了解一些真正有效的，有纪律性的温和教育方法，你的家庭将变得更加平静和快乐。想想在本章中我给你的工具。使用任何一个你觉得对你的家庭适合的。你的家人可能不完全需要他们，但请保持兴趣，在需要时他们说不定能平静的改变事情的结果。

如果当你被问到：很多家长不会把"尊重"与"孩子"关联起来，但其实这正是我们需要考虑的。尊重意味着"表现出尊敬或尊重他人的价值观或卓越感"。在我们的研讨会中有这样的练习，每次都会获得惊人的结果。我们有父母在课程的第三周左右开始跟着这些练习去做，所以每个人都能认识对方并且很愿意的分享。你也可以做到这一点;它直接与对人的尊重和对自己的自尊有关。

Silhouette Exercise

Imagine that there are two silhouettes of a child. Each one is on a separate piece of paper and they are black drawings on white paper. On one silhouette, write next to the drawing every bad thing that you can remember your parents said to you as you were growing up. You might write "stupid, lazy, worthless, not as cute as your sister…" There are a lot of terrible things people say to each other. You might have a few things written or maybe every bit of white space available is filled up. Now get a small sharp object, a pin or needle or toothpick. For every bad word said to you, and for every time it was said, poke a hole in the silhouette. Poke a hole in that child sitting next to all of those bad words.

Now wait, we aren't done. As if that wasn't bad enough, try this. Turn the paper over and smooth out all of those poke holes. Get them as smooth as possible. Turn it over again and look at it. Maybe it looks okay. Maybe you can barely see the holes. But, are they still there? Of course, they are. That is what we do to our children when we call them names or holler at them needlessly. We poke holes, permanent ones, in their very souls. My goal for this book is to get parents to think about not poking holes.

People in our workshops have been in tears, or shake their head in dismay as they remember things said to them. It is 15, 20 or 30 years later and it can still hurt like it happened two minutes ago.

> *Respectful Behavior*
>
> - *Show that you understand your child's feelings*
> - *Be firm, but fair*
> - *When disciplining, end on a positive note, "I know you can do better next time."*
> - *Walk away if you have to in order to avoid losing your temper*
> - *Be aware of personal space, let family members have some privacy*
> - *Limit teasing about personal attributes and abilities*
> - *Don't poke holes*

When you talk to your child about boundaries that have been broken, remember, no poked holes.

When someone calls you a name, they obviously are not being respectful. In order to earn the respect of our children we need to be role models, leaders in our homes. This means not calling each other names. How can we expect our children not to yell at each other when they hear yelling all the time? "Do as I say, not as I do," does not work. We are our children's first, and most important, role models. They will model our behavior. If we are respectful toward each other and them, they will know how to respect us right back.

The beauty of a respectful household is that it carries over into all aspects of life. I have had parents come up to me and say how their child's teacher has stated how pleasant their son or daughter is in class. Being respectful is not just about "please" and "thank you." It is about treating people as you would like to be treated. It is listening and learning, not judging or scolding.

Boundaries

Boundaries can be many things. They will be specific to your family and highlight what you see as important for your children to learn to become the terrific people you want them to be. Here are some issues to be discussed:

- Personal space

    o hitting, wrestling, tickling,
    o going into each other's rooms or backpacks

- o snooping in purses, phones, computers
- o have a discussion about what each family member considers to be private space

- Teasing/name calling
    - o What do you want your children to know about the hurt that comes from calling each other names?
    - o this might be necessary to unlearn from your own upbringing

- Being truthful
    - o lying always needs discussion and probably disciplining
    - o this is a very easy habit to get into if not handled
    - o remind kids that no one likes to be lied to

- Technology time
    - o how much is too much television time
    - o what are too many minutes on the phone
        - what will happen if children go over texting/phone minutes

- who gets the computer when

- Where are they?
  - as kids get older, you will need some parameters on when they need to let you know where they are going,
  - who are their friends, are parents home when they visit
  - curfews
  - phone call accessibility

Your initial discussions will be with the parents only. Boundaries will be set by you with additions and discussion involving the children later. They have input, but you, as parents, have the final say. It is interesting, however, to see how the children come up with disciplinary ideas if boundaries are broken. Often, they come up with harsher consequences for themselves and their siblings than you would yourselves.

Remember to be positive in how you present boundaries. Talk more about how you WANT them to act rather that how you don't want them to act. Avoid the word "punish" because it has such a harsh ring to it.

Encourage them and tell them that you are sure they will rarely cross these boundaries, even if little Jackie is in her biting stage. Being positive and setting high levels of behavior is how we raise great humans.

Discipline

In a perfect world, we would never have to do this. It is not easy telling a 3-year-old to sit still for 3 minutes because they just threw their sister's Barbies in the toilet. Believe me, that is easier than giving a time out to a 13-year-old as she throws up in the toilet from trying smoking or drinking with her buddies. And surprisingly, one thing certainly has something to do with another. By setting firm

> *Quick Tips*
> - Have a Parent Meeting to discuss boundaries and appropriate discipline if broken
> - Write up a short sheet to show the children
> - Have a Family Meeting to discuss new boundaries and consequences
> - Listen well and revise some things if necessary, but remember, the parents have to ultimate say for the family
> - Come back to the sheet periodically as the children grow and change or need reminders

boundaries, expectations and consequences when they are small, it is much easier for them to act well and make good decisions later. It is simple math. They will grow to understand that "Oh, if I do XXX, that will get me YYY so I won't be able to do ZZZ."

Here are some great ideas that work. Once you institute these disciplines/consequences your children will actually be less stressed because there are no surprises. And you will be amazed when they get ready to grab a toy from their sibling, think twice about it, (you might see smoke coming out of their ears as they process this) decide the timeout isn't worth it, and ask their sibling politely if they can have it next. Really happens, no kidding.

- Expressing disappointment
    - this works and a timeout may not be necessary for lesser events

- Timeouts
    - Gives them time to reflect
    - Needs to be in a not fun place
    - Age appropriate length of time

- Taking away privileges
    - Television, phone, computer, dessert, favorite restaurant
    - Use this for privileges only. Do not have them miss dinner or school sports etc.

When our children do something bad, or someone has crossed a boundary, aren't we disappointed in them? We might get angry and sad and frightened, but mostly, we think they are the nicest, brightest, best little beings in the world and we are heartily disappointed when they prove us wrong. It turns out most of them will make mistakes once in a while. Children do not like to disappoint their parents. They love basking in the glow of their love. Expressing disappointment is your first line of defense when boundaries have been crossed. The trick here is not to get angry or yell or scream. You will show on your face what your heart feels. Look horrified, look sad, tell them, "I am so disappointed in you. I thought you knew better." Parents do not need to go on and on and lecture and bore them to death with tales of woe. Just let them know how it makes you feel and wait for their reaction.

If we lecture they tune out, have time to come up with excuses and basically not care. By looking them in their pretty little eyes and show our disappointment without anger, believe me, they will feel badly. I don't want you to think that we are shaming them. You are just expressing your feelings. Often for minor problems, a quick, "Can you try your hardest not to do that again?" is enough to get everyone back on track. At that point, let it go, trust them and go back to your life, as they will.

This brings us to timeouts. This is a miracle cure for what ails the human species. Don't we all need timeouts once in a while? Don't we need time to reflect on what we have done or what the universe has thrust upon us? I think wars could have been avoided, murders not committed and divorces not granted if only people took more timeouts.

A friend of mine told me about her 4-year-old nephew. Her relatives were visiting from another country and had been staying with her for a month or so. She is a good parent and her own children were used to timeouts. The atmosphere in her household was calm, everyone knew what was expected of them and the chaos of raising four children was kept to a minimum. One day, her nephew dumped a huge bottle of liquid Tide down the carpeted stairs. He saw the damage and fearing his own behavior, the wrath of his mother and life in general, he ran screaming around the house, "I need a timeout, I need a timeout!" He had never had one before, but apparently noticed their efficacy. His auntie granted his wish and gave him an appropriate timeout, he said sorry and helped clean up the sudsy mess.

Some things to remember about timeouts are that they are not supposed to be fun and do not make them too long. It will do you no good to send your child to his or her own room if that is where all of their fun toys are.

Seasons

Have your child label each flap with the name of a season and use the inside to show what a tree looks like in winter, spring, summer and fall. Or, ask your child to list seasonal activities, months or holidays under the correct season

四季

让你的孩子用一个季节的名字标记每个标签,并使用里面的树来区别冬天,春天,夏天和秋天都有什么不一样。或者,要求小孩在正确的季节列出相对的季节性活动,月份或节日。

Hamburger

Fold a paper and have your child round off all four corners and color a delicious hamburger on the front. Your child can list his or her favorite hamburger ingredients, write the steps for making a hamburger, or describe a favorite **BBQ Party**.

汉堡包

折叠一张纸,让你的孩子四个角折起来,并在前面涂上一个美味的汉堡包。 你的孩子可以列出他或她最喜欢的汉堡包配料,写出制作汉堡包的步骤,或描述一个最喜欢的烧烤派对。

Present

With the fold at the bottom, have your child draw a gift box, complete with a bow and wrapping paper on the front of the fold-over. Inside ask your child to draw a picture and write about their favorite gift they have received.

礼物

让你的孩子在折纸的底部画一个礼物盒,然后把它用礼品纸包起来。让你的小孩在里面画一张照片,并写下他们想要收到的最喜爱的礼物。

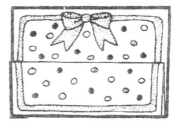

Cooking with Joseph

Don't let yourself be so concerned with raising a good child that you forget that you already have one.

Papi's Chili

Ingredients:

- ½ pound ground beef
- ½ pound ground pork
- 2 medium yellow onions
- 1 bunch of parsley
- 2 large cans diced tomatoes
- 1 pot of cooked bean (from Chapter One)
- 2 small cans of kidney beans
- ¼ cup butter
- Salt to taste
- Pepper to taste
- Cayenne pepper (or any chili powder)
-

Direction:

- Mix cooked beans, tomatoes and kidney beans in a large pot and heat on medium

- In medium skillet sauté ¼ of yellow onion with a tablespoon of butter
  Add ground beef to sautéed onions and brown adding salt, pepper to taste

- In another medium skillet sauté ¼ of yellow onion with a tablespoon of butter

Add ground pork to sautéed onions and brown adding salt and pepper to taste.

- Once both meats have been browned, drain excess fat and place in pot with beans

- In medium skillet sauté chopped onions with 1/8 cup of butter. Once onions are translucent add them to pot of beans

- In medium skillet sauté chopped parsley with 1/8 cup of butter. Once parsley has softened add to the pot of beans

- Add chili powder, salt and pepper to taste and let it all simmer on low heat for 1 hour

Cornbread

Ingredients:

- 6 tablespoons unsalted butter, melted
  1 cup cornmeal
- ¾ cup all-purpose flour
- 1 tablespoon sugar
- 1 ½ teaspoon baking powder
- ½ teaspoon baking soda
- ¼ teaspoon salt
- 2 large eggs
- 1 ½ cups buttermilk

Direction:

- Preheat the oven to 425° F.

- Lightly grease an 8-inch baking dish.

- In a large bowl, mix together the cornmeal, flour, sugar, baking powder, baking soda, and salt

- In a separate bowl, mix together the eggs, buttermilk and butter

- Pour the buttermilk mixture into the cornmeal mixture and fold together until there are no dry spots (the batter will still be lumpy).

- Pour the batter into the prepared baking dish.

- Bake until the top is golden brown and tester inserted into the middle of the corn bread comes out clean, about 20 to 25 minutes.

- Remove the cornbread from the oven and let it cool for 10 minutes before serving.

Banana Pudding

Ingredients:

- 1 box instant vanilla pudding
- 2 medium bananas
- 1 12 oz. semi-sweet chocolate chips

Directions:

- Combine instant pudding with 3 cups cold milk and mix for 4 minutes until firm

- Place pudding in refrigerator for 5 minutes

- Cut bananas into 1/8-inch slices

- Combine chocolate chips and bananas with pudding and serve

- Can be served over a light pound cake

Epilogue
Season everything with love and encouragement

When I was 15 years old, my father came home and gave me an article from the Los Angeles Times that contained a recipe. The article was about how Elizabeth Taylor, while filming, *Cleopatra,* in Rome, ordered Chasen's Famous Chili from Chasen's Restaurant in Beverly Hills to be sent to her on dry ice. Over the years I have modified the recipe and it has become a tradition for my son, Joseph and I to cook it when the weather turns cold.

My father recognized my passion for cooking and knew that I would rejoice when given the opportunity to try a new recipe. He payed attention to the clues and knew what I was interested in, even when it did not interest him. He did not downplay my interests, but rather encouraged my dreams. To this day cooking brings me joy and is therapeutic for me.

Cooking is my passion and I have had the opportunity to share my passion with my children while building a stronger relationship with them. Your passion may be different, but whatever it is, share it with your children and you, too, will build long lasting bonds. I would also remind you to be a cheerleader for your children and encourage their gifts and passions. Allow your children to explore and dream and discover their passions.

This book is one in a series of books in which I share my experiences and thoughts on raising great kids. It is designed for readers to take the suggestions and practice them at home with their children remembering that each one is an individual and has his or her own unique talents and gifts. Just as I have modified the Chasen's recipe you should modify these suggestions to meet your kid's needs. And I wish you the best of luck on cooking up some new experiences with your children! Happy Cooking!

About the Author:

Gary Surdam is an educator, entrepreneur, businessman and visionary whose unique career experience has made him one of American's top leaders in educational consulting.

After 13 years of classroom teaching experience, and having dealt first-had with obstacles to learning and literacy, he realized that simply "following the lesson plan" wasn't enough to create a spirit of lifelong learning. Surdam developed a vision of empowering parents, teachers and school administrators to help children succeed in school and life. He called his vision "The Bright Start Way".

Gary Surdam's innovations have united business and education to make academic success a reality for students, teachers and administrators throughout the nation. He continues to share this vision, providing access to the heart of education and helping other people reach their potential in academics and in life.

Visit: www.brightstartparentworkshops.com

Made in the USA
Monee, IL
01 June 2025

18494472R00075